Wales

small country - big history

Sarah Curtius

Bibliografische Information der Deutschen
Nationalbibliothek:

Die Deutsche Nationalbibliothek verzeichnet diese Publikation in der Deutschen National-
bibliografie; detaillierte bibliografische Daten sind im Internet über
http://dnb.dnb.de abrufbar.

Herstellung und Verlag: BoD – Books on Demand,
Norderstedt

ISBN: 978-3-75-786278-7

CONTENTS

INTRODUCTION

What do people think of when they think of Wales?

Maybe you think about rugby, or about male voice choirs, or about sheep on the rolling green hills, or about a strange language on the road signs. Maybe you think of famous Welsh people like the singer Tom Jones or the actress Catherine Zeta Jones or the footballer Gareth Bale.

Maybe you don't think of anything at all. Maybe you don't know anything about Wales. Or maybe you think such a small country cannot be very important.

Wales is a small country. It is just over 20,000 km^2 which is 17 times smaller than Germany. And just over 3.2 million people live in Wales.

The story of Wales has sometimes been told as the story of a land invaded by other nations who took the resources to make themselves rich but treated the Welsh badly. As you will see in the stories in the book, this was sometimes true. Especially in the period of industrialisation, a few families came to Wales and became very rich. The Marquis of Bute came from Scotland and became the richest man in the world in the 19th century by transporting coal through the docks in Cardiff. The Crayshaw family came from Yorkshire in England and became rich from the iron industry. The Vivian family from Cornwall made their wealth in Swansea's copper industry.

However, this is only part of the story. As you will soon see, Wales has always been at the centre of world history, trading with neighbours and shaping the world we live in.

In this book you will not read stories about the rich and famous foreigners who made their money in Wales. Instead, you will read about Welsh people who changed the world in some way. Some of them are famous. Some of them, you will probably never have heard of. I hope you find them interesting.

In addition, I want to give you some idea of what to expect if you decide to visit this beautiful country. You will find mountains, hills, valleys and rivers, a long coastline and lots of activities to do outdoors. You will also find a country full of history, with hundreds of castles, ancient churches and museums.

Also, as we have already mentioned, you will find out about a country which has its own ancient language and that is what I would like to begin with! We are going to start by learning some Welsh! Below are some phrases you can use on a trip to Wales. The language may look unusual but I have given you some help with the pronunciation. Have a try and enjoy learning about this wonderful country!

Bore da (Pronounced: Boh-reh dah)   **Good morning**

Prynhawn da (Prin-hawn dah)   **Good afternoon**

Nos da (nohs dah)   **Good night**

Croeso i Gymru (Croesoh ee Gum-reeh)   **Welcome to Wales**

Iechyd da! (Yeh-chid dah)   **Good health! (Cheers!)**

Diolch (Dee-olch)   **Thanks**

Da iawn (Dah ee-aw-n)   **Very good**

United Kingdom

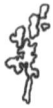

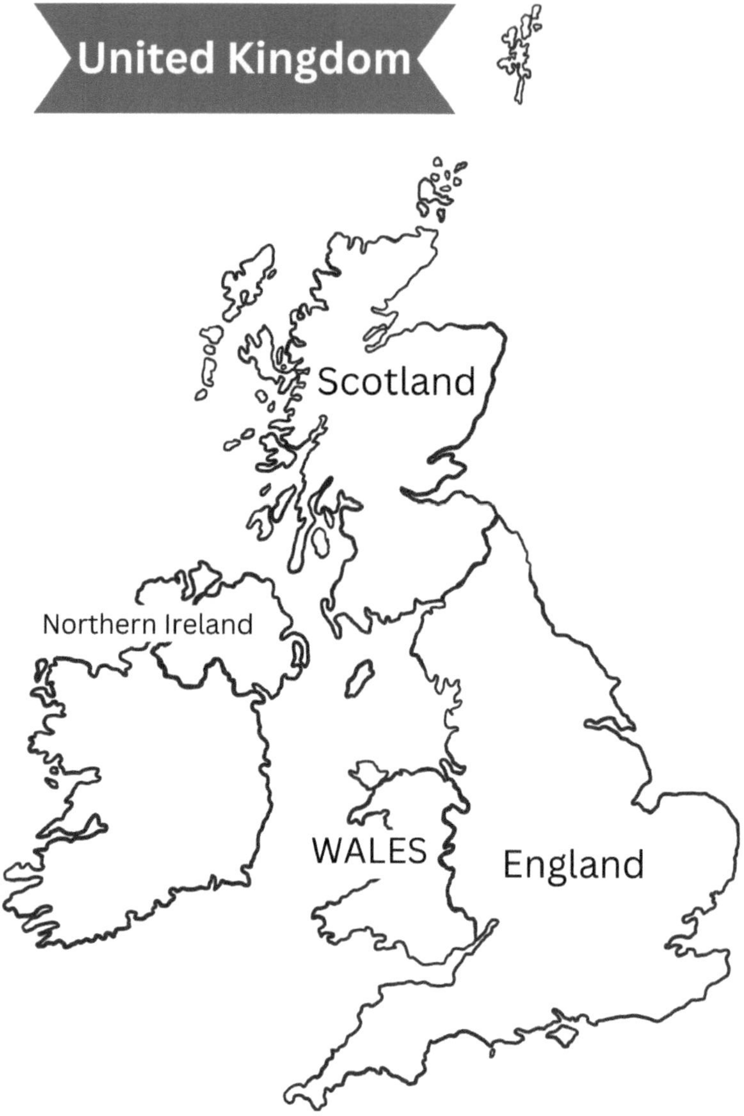

Scotland
Northern Ireland
WALES
England

PREHISTORIC
WALES

Pentre Ifan,
in Preseli Hills,
Pembrokeshire

Stonehenge,
Wiltshire,
England

PREHISTORIC WALES

Stonehenge, South England

You may be surprised to see a photograph of Stonehenge at the beginning of a book about Wales. Stonehenge is a stone circle on the Salisbury Plain in Wiltshire, south England. Stonehenge consists of two stone circles. The outer circle is made of stones taken from the local area. However, the inner circle is made of bluestones which came from the Preseli Hills in the south-west corner of Wales.

In 2018, archaeologists discovered that, not only were the stones cut from the Preseli hills, they had, in fact, already stood there as a stone circle. The scientists believe that the people who lived in west Wales moved to Wiltshire around 3,000 BC and took their monument with them. How they managed to transport these enormous stones the 270 kilometres to Stonehenge is still a mystery.

In this chapter we take a look at Wales in the prehistoric period. We'll find out about a young man mistaken for a woman, an unbelievable Bronze Age industry and who the Celts were and where they came from. The travel tip is the officially named "Area of Outstanding Natural Beauty", the Gower peninsula.

THE RED LADY OF PAVILAND

In December 1822, William Buckland received an interesting parcel from Lady Mary Cole who lived on the Gower Peninsula in south Wales. The parcel contained what seemed to be an elephant's skull and tusk found in a cave in Paviland, near Lady Mary's home.

Buckland was the first Professor of Geology at Oxford University and was very interested by the find. In January 1823, he made his way to the cave at Paviland to see what else was there. Buckland found some human bones which had been dyed red with ochre, a natural dye. As well as the bones, he also found lots of shells and ivory which had also been dyed red. Buckland had a number of different ideas about the bones. He decided they must have belonged to a woman, because he believed the shells had been part of a necklace. He thought she must have been a witch or a prostitute who lived about 2,000 years earlier, when the Romans were in Britain. He called the bones the "Red Lady of Paviland".

However, when the bones were studied properly, scientists discovered that they belonged to a young man between 25 and 30 years old. In 2008, modern radiocarbon dating showed that the bones were much older than Buckland thought. In fact, the young man lived 33,000 years ago during a slightly warmer period of the last Ice Age.

The "elephant" skull and the ivory were actually from a mammoth. Many more animal bones and stone tools were found in the cave. The young man and others with him were probably hunting mammoth and other animals in the area where he was buried. Nowadays, the cave is close to the sea and can only be reached in the winter low tides[1]. However, when the young man was alive, it was at least 110 kilometres away from the sea and the area was full of bison, reindeer, woolly mammoths and woolly rhinos.

The red bones of the "Red Lady of Paviland" form one of the earliest ritual burials[2] ever found in Western Europe.

---

1. tide = the way the sea level rises and falls during the day

2. ritual burial = burying a person according to a special ceremony

COPPER MONOPOLY

Pentre Ifan

The last Ice Age drove humans, like the tribe the "Red Lady" belonged to, from Britain. It ended around 10,000 BC and people once again returned from central Europe to live in Britain. Stone Age people left their mark on the landscape in Wales, building small settlements and creating stone monuments like the burial chamber at Pentre Ifan.

As Britain moved from the Stone Age into the Bronze Age (around 2,000 BC), Wales was to play an important role. Bronze is made from copper and tin. Both of those metals could be easily found in Britain at the time and we now know that, for a few hundred years, one mine in the north-west of Wales provided almost all of Britain's copper.

The Great Orme is part of the headland[1] near the Victorian seaside town of Llandudno. At the same time Stonehenge was being moved to Salisbury Plain, people began digging the eight-kilometre-long tunnels on the Great Orme in order to mine copper. Some of the tunnels are so narrow, scientists believe they must have been dug by small children of about five years old.

The workers used stones from the beach and animal bones to dig the copper ore. 3,000 stone hammers and other tools have been found at the site.

When the first tunnels were discovered in 1987, it was thought that this was a small local mine. However, researchers have discovered that between 1600 and 1400 BC, the mine on the Great Orme was the main source of copper in Britain. Copper from the mine was traded throughout Europe and objects made of copper from the Great Orme have been found in France, the Netherlands and Sweden.

In 2005, the Great Orme Copper Mines were named 'The Largest Prehistoric Copper Mines in the World' by the Guinness Book of World Records.

---

1. a high piece of land at the coast

THE WELSH LANGUAGE I

THE ARRIVAL OF THE CELTS

Celtic Village

In the 20th century, people believed that the Celts were a group of tribes from central Europe which invaded the British Isles several times around 500 BC. However, modern researchers suggest that Celtic tribes started to arrive much earlier. It is believed that they were not part of a violent invasion, but Celts who came to trade and then settled with the people already living in the British Isles.

The Celts who settled in what is now Wales and the south of England came from Armorica. Readers of the Asterix comics may recognise this name. It is the home of Asterix and Obelix which we now know as Brittany in the north-west of France. They began coming to Britain and Ireland as early as 5,000 BC.

The contact to the British Isles became more intense in the Bronze Age because Britain had both copper and tin which everyone in Europe was looking for. There was not as much contact between Britain and Europe in the Iron Age because iron could be found everywhere in Europe.

By the time the Romans arrived, there were a number of different Celtic tribes living in Britain. They fought each other and had their own individual gods. However, they were united by a common culture and language. The people spoke "Brythonic" which developed into Welsh. It is the Welsh language which defined the people who lived in Wales for centuries and is still spoken today.

VISIT WALES I

THE GOWER PENINSULA

A peninsula is a long piece of land almost completely surrounded by water. The Gower peninsula is on the south coast of Wales, near the city of Swansea. It was the first area in the United Kingdom to be called an "Area of Outstanding Natural Beauty". It has woods, long golden beaches with clear blue water and high dramatic cliffs.

There are lots of beautiful beaches to visit on the Gower. Some, like **Caswell**, **Langland** and **Oxwich** have car parks, toilets and cafés where you can buy an ice cream.

If you do not mind walking down to the beach, **Three Cliffs Bay** is a good tip. The three big cliffs shelter the lovely sandy bay. It is always quiet and you might be able to watch some surfers on this beach.

If you like hiking, you can follow the coast path across the cliffs and past the pretty beaches in the south and through the salt marshes in the north. There are plenty of pubs where you can find something to eat and drink on the way.

The cave in Paviland is difficult to reach, but there are other historical sites to discover, like the Stone Age monument Arthur's Stone and a number of castle ruins from different periods.

At the furthest end of the peninsula is **Rhossili** beach and Worm's Head. Rhossili is often in the top ten of the world's best beaches. The walk down to the long sandy beach is quite steep and will feel longer on the way back up! However, it is worth it and, even on a warm sunny day in the middle of summer, you will have the beach almost to yourself.

The rocky island of Worm's Head can be reached on foot two hours before and two hours after low tide. Check the times before you set off – many people have had a longer a stay than planned on this little island!

Myths & Legends

Ynys Llanddwyn,
Anglesey

Beddgelert,
Snowdonia

Myths and Legends

A number of the organisations which promote Welsh tourism call Wales the "land of myths and legends". In this chapter you will read a few of the famous stories and legends which shape the way the Welsh see themselves. The first story is about the red dragon which you can see on the flag flown everywhere in Wales. The second story is the tragic tale of the faithful dog Gelert and the final story is about the Welsh saint of love.

You will also find out about words in Welsh for the landscape and what to visit in the stunning national park of Snowdonia.

THE RED DRAGON

The Welsh flag has a red dragon on a white and green background. There are only three flags which have a dragon on them: Wales, Bhutan and Malta (it's very small but it is there!). So why does the Welsh flag have a dragon?

There is a legend about a 5th century Celtic ruler called Vortigern who was fighting the Saxons. He wanted to build a castle in what is now north Wales. He had found the perfect spot and started the work but every morning the builders found the walls had been knocked down.

A young boy from Caer Myrddin (in English, Carmarthen) told Vortigern why this was happening. He said, there were two dragons, a red one and a white one. They were asleep in a lake in the mountain. Vortigern told his workers to dig into the mountain and there they found the dragons as the boy had said, asleep in an underground lake.

When the workers let the water out of the lake, the dragons started to fight. The red dragon won and the white dragon fled. The red dragon went back to his home in the mountain and Vortigern could build his castle which he called Dinas Emrys after the boy. In Welsh, the boy's name is Myrddin Emrys. In English, he is usually called Merlin. You may have heard about Merlin from the stories about King Arthur and the Knights of the Round Table.

The red dragon is a symbol for the Celts and the white dragon is a symbol for the Saxons.

So, did Vortigern and his castle really exist? In 1945, archaeologists dug at Dinas Emrys. They found underground water and the walls of the castle which had been rebuilt several times.

From the legend to the modern flag ...

In the Hundred Years War with France, English kings used a flag with a red dragon because Welsh soldiers were in the army and helped to defeat the French by using their longbows.

A flag with a red dragon was used in the final battle of the War of the Roses. Henry Tudor was fighting at the head of the Lancaster army against King Richard III and his York army. Henry Tudor was born in

Wales and beat Richard III at the battle of Bosworth Field in 1485. You'll read more about King Henry VII later in the book.

The flag with the red dragon did not become the official Welsh flag until the 20th century. In 1801, the Union flag was created when the Kingdom of Great Britain (Scotland and England) and the Kingdom of  Ireland were joined. The flag included St George's Cross for England (a red cross on a white background), St Andrew's Cross for Scotland (a diagonal white cross on a blue background) and a different style of St George's Cross for Ireland (a diagonal red cross on a white background). The red dragon was not included because, in the 19th century, Wales was not seen as a separate country from England.

However, in 1969, Queen Elizabeth established the flag as the official flag of Wales which was to be flown from government buildings in Wales. Today the Welsh flag with the red dragon is EVERYWHERE in Wales! Welsh people fly it with great pride.

BEDDGELERT

One of the best-known Welsh legends is about Prince Llywelyn and his dog Gelert.

Beddgelert Village

The Welsh Prince Llywelyn the Great and his family lived in a palace in Gwynedd, north Wales. He had a faithful hunting dog called Gelert which was a gift from King John of England.

One day, Llywelyn and his wife went hunting and left his baby son with a nurse and servant. After some time, Llywelyn noticed that Gelert was missing. The party returned to the palace and the dog came out to meet them. He was wagging his tail but he was covered in blood.

Llywelyn went inside and found the baby's bed was turned over and the bedclothes were covered in blood. Llywelyn was filled with anger and killed his dog. The dog made a noise before he died and then Llywelyn heard the baby crying. He found his baby son unhurt but next to him was the body of a dead wolf. The dog had killed the wolf to save the baby.

Llywelyn buried the dog in a field and covered the grave with a pile of stones called a cairn. The village where this happened is called Beddgelert which means Gelert's grave.

Saint Dwynwen

Island Llanddwyn

Romantic Welsh people have two days in the year to celebrate romantic love. As well as St Valentine's Day, the Welsh celebrate Saint Dwynwen as the patron saint of love.

Dwynwen's father, King Brychan had 24 daughters. He arranged a marriage for Dwynwen with a prince, but she was in love with a local man called Maelon. Maelon was very unhappy and Dwynwen ran into the woods to cry and pray to God. An angel visited Dwynwen and gave her a potion. The potion was supposed to make her forget Maelon but it also turned Maelon into a block of ice.

God gave Dwynwen three wishes. Firstly, she wished that Maelon be saved and not be a block of ice anymore. Secondly, she asked God to help all true lovers. Thirdly, she asked to remain unmarried for the rest of her life.

She went to the island of Anglesey and founded a convent on the island which is now called Llanddwyn. Her saint's day is celebrated on January 25th.

THE WELSH LANGUAGE II

PLACE NAMES

Places in Wales often have two names – a Welsh one and an English one. Knowing a little bit of the Welsh language can tell you a lot about the countryside. Here are some examples:

- **Caer** means fort or castle (e.g., Caerdydd, the Welsh name for Cardiff)

- **Aber** means the mouth of a river (e.g., Abertawe, the Welsh name for Swansea where the River Tawe flows into the sea)

- Places that begin with **Llan** are very common in Wales. **Llan** means a place with a church (e.g., Llanddwyn which we read about in the last chapter. Llanelli is another one of hundreds of examples! The Welsh have a lot of churches!). The "ll" sound in Welsh does not exist in English. To say "ll", you put the tip of your tongue behind your teeth as if you wanted to pronounce "l". Then you blow air out of the sides of your mouth. Easy!

- Wales also has a lot of rivers, so you will find places that start with **rhyd** (meaning ford, a shallow part of a river where you can cross on foot or in a wagon ... or car today) or **pont**, meaning bridge.

- **Bryn** means hill and **cwm** means valley

Road signs in Wales have both the English and Welsh names on them. People in Wales are becoming worried that the traditional Welsh place names are being lost because people only use the English names. In November 2022, the Snowdon National Park decided that they would change the park's name to Eryri and the mountain Snowdon would now be called by its Welsh name, Yr Wyddfa.

In April 2023, the National Park in south Wales announced they would also use the Welsh name for the park. It is now called Bannau Brycheiniog.

Visit Wales II

Snowdonia / Eryri

Snowdonia is a national park in the north of Wales. The park has fifteen mountains which are over 1,000 metres high. Almost one fifth of the park is woodland and there are many mountain farms.

The highest mountain in the park is **Yr Wyddfa**, or, in English, Snowdon. 600,000 people visit Snowdon every year and on sunny days there is even a queue at the top of the mountain. On a clear day, you can see Ireland, the Isle of Man and even as far as the Lake District in the north of England. Some Welsh people joke that this is a good reason not to go up Snowdon on a clear day!

People should not think that climbing Snowdon is easy. The mountain is not very high compared to the Alps, for example. However, Snowdonia is close to the sea and the weather can change very suddenly. Sir Edmund Hilary and his team practiced climbing Snowdon before they became the first people to climb Everest.

For those who do not want to walk to the top, they can take the Snowdon Mountain Railway. It was built in 1896 and is one of the most beautiful train journeys in the world. The carriages are pushed to the top either by a diesel engine or a traditional steam engine.

There has always been a strong Welsh-speaking community in Snowdonia. 58% of the people who live in the national park speak Welsh as their first language. Schools in the area use Welsh as the language for teaching.

Beddgelert is within the National Park and there are many other myths and legends connected to the area. The Welsh name for Snowdon itself, Yr Wyddfa comes from a legend about the giant Rhita Gawr. According to the legend, the giant fought King Arthur and was buried under a pile of stones on the top of the mountain. The Welsh word "gwyddfa" means grave. Yr Wyddfa is pronounced "er-with-va".

THE AGE OF SAINTS

Celtic Cross in Nevern,
Pembrokeshire

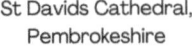

St Davids Cathedral,
Pembrokeshire

THE AGE OF SAINTS

Celtic Cross in Nevern

In this chapter you will meet Wales's patron saint, Saint David and see how important the Celtic saints were in Wales. You can learn about the Celtic saints who built churches like this one in Nevern. The church in Nevern was founded in the 6th century and there is a stone in the churchyard from this time. The cross in the photograph is from the late 10th century and nearby are ancient yew trees which are 700 years old. There are many sites in Pembrokeshire in west Wales where the Celtic saints left their mark and that is the travel tip for this chapter.

CHRISTIANITY IN WALES

It is well known that Julius Caesar led an invasion of Britain in 55 BC. However, his invasion was unsuccessful and it was not until 100 years later that Emperor Claudius established Britain as a Roman province. Some of the Celtic tribes chose to fight the Romans, for example, the Iceni tribe led by Boudica in 60 AD. Boudica and her army were defeated by the smaller but better trained Romans.

Other Celtic tribes chose to make peace with the Romans and Britain became a successful and mostly peaceful province. The Romans left their mark on Britain in many ways. They built roads, forts, villas, amphitheatres, and baths. During the Roman occupation, a unique culture developed which was a mixture of Roman and Celtic influences.

The Romans also brought their Christian faith which developed into a Celtic Christianity. The Celtic Christians used images from nature to explain the religion to the people. They made large stone crosses with complex patterns and the monks created beautiful manuscripts like the Book of Kells[1].

Celtic saints preached throughout Europe. Saint Patrick went to Ireland, Saint Boniface to the Franks in what is now Germany and Saint Gallen in what is now Switzerland.

By 410, the Roman troops were called back to Europe and the occupation of Britain ended. Anglcs and Saxons invaded and settled in the south east of Britain and many Celts fled to areas in the west.

Saint Illytd established a centre for learning in Llantwit Major, near modern day Cardiff. Some of the most famous Welsh saints are said to have studied there, including Saint Samson who later lived and preached in Brittany in France, and Wales's patron saint, David.

---

1. The Book of Kells is a copy of the four gospels with beautiful artwork. It was made around 800 AD and can be seen in Trinity College in Dublin.

Saint David

Wales's Patron Saint

St Davids Cathedral

David was born around 500 AD in the south-west of Wales. His name in Welsh is Dafydd or Dewi. David trained as a priest and travelled in the west of England, in Brittany and in Wales. He founded 12 monasteries in south Wales. In 550, he founded a monastery near the city now called St Davids. His monks lived very simple lives. They worked in the fields and prayed. They drank only water and milk and ate no meat.

There are many legends about David. In one story, he preached to a large crowd. The people thought that they would not be able to hear and see him but the ground underneath David rose and soon he was standing on a hill. Now everyone could see and hear him. While he was preaching, a dove landed on his shoulder. In paintings of David, he is usually standing on a hill with a dove on his shoulder. His last words were "Be joyful, keep the faith, do the little things you have seen me do".

David was buried in the city which now carries his name. In 1081, the first Norman king, William the Conqueror visited St Davids to pray. More and more people travelled to St Davids to pray and soon they needed a bigger cathedral. In the Middle Ages, two pilgrimages to St Davids were equal to one pilgrimage to Rome and three were equal to one to Jerusalem. In 1181, work began on the cathedral we see today.

St David is the patron saint of Wales and he is celebrated on the 1st March. On this day, Welsh people wear a leek or a daffodil. Children go to school in traditional dress and there are concerts and evenings to celebrate Welsh language and culture.

daffodil & leek

The Welsh Language III

Foreign Influences

When different cultures and languages meet, there is always some mixing that takes place. Over the centuries, Romans, Anglo-Saxons, Vikings and Normans all came to Wales and some left their mark on the language.

The Romans ruled Britain for centuries. Their administration was done in Latin. There are a number of words in Welsh which come from Latin. This is often because the Romans introduced something for which the Welsh did not have a word.

The Romans brought Christianity and with that came churches (Latin ecclesia; Welsh **eglwys**) and lots of vocabulary for religion and church. We also have windows (**ffenestr** in Welsh) and bridges (**pont**) which the Romans introduced, as well as **castell** (castle or fort) and **mur** (wall). The words for people (**pobl**) and children (**plant**) also come from Latin, as does a very important word in modern Wales – the **senedd** which means parliament.

There are some modern English words which are used in Welsh, sometimes with a different spelling to show Welsh pronunciation. Here are some examples. Can you work out what they are?

- tacsi

- ambwlans

- car

- ffôn

- siop

- coffi

(Clues: Welsh has no letter "x"; "w" is pronounced like "u"; "si" is pronounced like "sh")

You can see the answers on page 118.

Welsh has also given some words to English. Examples are **bard** (a poet), **coracle** (a small round boat) and, most famously, **corgi** which in Welsh literally means "dwarf dog". Queen Elizabeth's favourite dogs are originally from Pembrokeshire.

Visit Wales III

Pembrokeshire

St Davids is the smallest city in the UK with around 1,800 inhabitants.[1] The cathedral is in a grassy valley on the site of Saint David's origi-

---

1. Until the 19th century, a city was defined as a town with a cathedral. Nowadays larger towns without a cathedral can apply to become cities.

nal monastery. The cathedral we see today was built in the late 12th century when it was recognised as a place of pilgrimage. In the 13th century, the tower collapsed and there was also an earthquake but the cathedral survived.

The cathedral tower has a wooden frame for bells but the cathedral was built on wet ground and the bells were too heavy. In the 1930s, the 13th century octagonal Bell Tower was repaired and strengthened and it now has a "ring" of ten bells.

Next to the cathedral are the ruins of the Bishop's Palace. This was a very impressive palace in the 14th century but it started to fall into ruin when the lead was removed from the roof in the 16th century.

The city of St Davids is not far from the sea and the beautiful coastal path. Near St Davids, the path passes the ancient ruins of **Saint Non's chapel**. Saint Non was Saint David's mother and the chapel is believed to be one of the oldest Christian buildings in Wales. In the chapel, you can find a large stone with a Celtic cross on it. It was found in the field near the chapel and was made sometime between the 7th and 9th century.

There is another chapel in Pembrokeshire which is worth a visit – **St Govan's chapel**. The chapel was built on the spot where it is believed the Irish saint Govan lived in the 5th and 6th centuries. The chapel you see now was built about 800 years ago, although the stone altar inside the chapel is much older.

The chapel can only be reached via stone steps from the Pembrokeshire Coastal Path and there are beautiful views from here. This part of the coastal path goes through land used by the British Army and walkers should check whether it is open before setting off. You don't want to get shot at!

WALES IN THE MIDDLE AGES

Coronation of King
Harold 1066,
Bayeux Tapestry

Caerphilly Castle,
South Wales

WALES IN THE MIDDLE AGES

One of the most important dates in British history is 1066. This is the year that the Norman lord William invaded England and won the battle against the Anglo-Saxon king Harold at Hastings. He became William I, usually known as William the Conqueror.

In this chapter, we will meet some of the medieval heroes of the Welsh people: Hywel Dda, Llywelyn the Great and Llywelyn the Last. You will also read about some amazing Welsh women called Gwenllian and Nest. However, this is also the period when Wales changed from being an independent nation with a growing sense of what it means to be Welsh into a country ruled by invaders. The Norman king Edward I, his son who received the title "The Prince of Wales" and his Norman lords all tried to control the Welsh.

Wales has more castles than any other country on earth – over 600! Some were built by the Welsh to keep invaders out. Some were built by the invaders to keep the Welsh out! Our travel tip looks at some of these impressive castles.

HYWEL DDA (890-950)

One of the most important Welsh rulers of the Middle Ages was Hywel Dda (Hywel the Good). Through his marriage to the daughter of the King of Dyfed as well as his ruthlessness, he took control of three quarters of modern Wales.

In 928, Hywel became the first Welsh prince to go on a pilgrimage to Rome. On his return, Hywel made an alliance with the Anglo-Saxon King of Wessex, Athelstan which helped strengthen his position.

Hywel is most well-known for the laws published in his name. Legend says that Hywel called expert lawyers and priests together to collect and codify the laws of Wales. The laws were unusual for their time. They covered a range of everyday matters, like marriage, property rights and inheritance. Instead of punishment[1], the laws focused on restorative justice. This means that the laws did not simply punish

---

1. punishment = treatment of someone who has done something wrong or broken the law

people who had done wrong, but tried to reconcile[2] the wrong-doer with the victim.

For example, there was no punishment for someone who had stolen food in order to survive. Often the "punishment" for hurting someone was the payment of compensation to the victim. If you cut off someone's finger, you had to pay 80 pence. For a thumb, it was 180 pence because the person would no longer be able to grip a weapon or farming equipment.

In Welsh law, women had far more rights than in other societies in the Middle Ages. There were only three reasons a man could beat his wife – if she was found with another man, if she gave away something she should not have, or if she wished a mark on her husband's beard (!). If she was beaten for any other reason, she could demand compensation.

There were also differences in the understanding of marriage. The first seven years of a marriage were a trial period. If the couple decided to separate before this time, they could do so and their belongings were divided between them 50/50.

Under Welsh law, illegitimate[3] children had the same rights as legitimate children. While this seems fair, it caused problems for rulers who had many sons. In the centuries after Hywel Dda, we see again and again that territories were split into smaller parts, making it more difficult to form a territory ruled by one powerful ruler, as was the case in England.

---

2. reconcile = to bring people who are not speaking to each other back together again

3. illegitimate = a child is illegitimate if their parents are not married

This is what happened directly after Hywel's death. His land was divided into three parts. However, his laws were used in Wales for three centuries until the death of the last prince of Wales, Llywelyn ap Grufudd in 1292.

THE MARCHER LORDS

Caerphilly Castle

When William of Normandy came to Britain and became William I, he brought with him a large number of ambitious lords. Having supported William, they now wanted to be rewarded with land in the new country. For the Norman king, this was a way to make sure that the country could be controlled by the new power. Norman lords were given land along the border between Wales and England and along the south coast all the way to the Irish Sea. Another word for border region was "march" and these local rulers were called "Marcher Lords".

In England, the new Norman lords were not allowed to build castles. Only the king could do that. However, in Wales, the lords were allowed to build castles and keep small armies to be able to control the local population. The areas controlled by the Norman lords were called "Marchia Wallia" while the areas controlled by the Welsh were called "Pura Wallia".

MEDIEVAL WELSH WOMEN

GWENLLIAN AND NEST

Gwenllian (1100-1136)

Gwenllian was the youngest daughter of Gruffydd ap Cynan (1055–1137) who was the Prince of Gwynedd in the north. She was said to be very beautiful and when Gruffydd ap Rhys, Prince of Deheubarth visited her father, he fell in love with his teenage daughter. The two ran away and married. They had eight children.

Gwenllian lived with her family in Deheubarth in south-west Wales where they were fighting with Norman, Anglo-Saxon and Flemish invaders who were trying to establish colonies in the area. It is said that she and her husband stole goods and money from the settlers and shared it out to the Welsh, like "Robin Hoods" of Wales.

In 1135, the Norman ruler Stephen made himself king instead of his cousin Mathilda which threw England into civil war. Seeing this as a chance to recover some of their lands, the Welsh rulers started attacks on the Normans in 1136.

Gwenllian's husband travelled to her father to form an alliance to fight the Normans. While he was away, the Normans attacked and Gwenllian led her army to fight them. In a battle near Kidwelly Castle, her army was defeated by the Normans and Gwenllian was captured and beheaded, along with two of her sons.

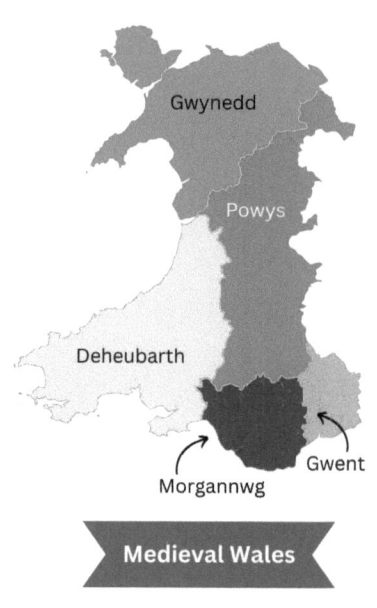

Medieval Wales

Gwenllian is the only medieval Welsh woman to lead an army into battle. For centuries after her death, Welsh soldiers would shout "Revenge[1] for Gwenllian" before battles with the Normans.

---

1. revenge = something you do to someone who has harmed you

Nest (1085-1136)

Gwenllian's sister-in-law, Gruffydd's sis-
ter had a very different relationship
with the Normans. Their father, Rhys ap
Tewdwr was the last King of Deheubarth.
He died in battle against the Normans in
1093 and Nest was taken hostage[2] . There
she met the future King Henry I and had
a child by him.

In 1105, Nest married Gerald of Windsor,
a Norman knight who was given control
of Pembroke Castle. Nest and Gerald had
at least five children.

She was a beautiful woman and a cousin
of hers called Owain, the son of the Prince of Powys wanted to meet
her. At Christmas 1109, he came to Gerald's castle (Carew Castle). He
later attacked the castle and set it on fire. In the confusion, Gerald
escaped out of a privy hole (where the waste from the toilet went) and
Owain kidnapped Nest and two of her sons. This angered both the
Normans and the other Welsh princes and civil war broke out.

Gerald died a year later. Nest married a second time and had more
children. She died around 1136.

One of her and Gerald's sons became Bishop of Wales and she is the
grandmother of Gerald of Wales, the great medieval writer.

---

2. hostage = a person who is kept as a prisoner, often because the
   person keeping them wants money or something else

LLYWELYN THE GREAT AND LLYWELYN THE LAST PRINCE OF WALES

Llywelyn the Great (1173-1240)

Llywelyn the Great ruled Gwynedd in the north from 1200 and 1240. Llywelyn became more and more powerful until he was recognised by the other Welsh princes as their overlord and they paid him tribute. Llywelyn made an agreement with King John[1] and married Joan, one of John's illegitimate daughters (although he already had a Welsh wife).

Llywelyn built castles like the Normans and also conquered castles built by the Marcher lords in the south of Wales.

---

1. King John was a very weak king. He is known as John Lackland because, after many wars in France, he lost the lands in France which belonged to the English king. His barons were so angry because the war with France was so expensive that, in 1215, they made him sign the Magna Carta which gave them more rights.

Llywelyn the Last (1223-1282)

Llywelyn's son with the English princess Joan was called Dafydd and Llywelyn made him ruler before he died. Dafydd imprisoned his older half-brother Gruffydd who was Llywelyn's son with his Welsh partner. When Dafydd was called to pay homage to the new English King Henry III, Henry put Gruffydd in the Tower of London.

On St David's Day 1244, Gruffydd tried to escape. Sadly, his rope broke as he climbed out of a window and he died. Dafydd also died two years later without an heir.

Gruffydd had four sons. Llywelyn was the second son. He was in Gwynedd when his uncle Dafydd died. He too had to fight his brothers but he won and took power. He took control of west and mid Wales and by encouraging the local people to support him, he gave the people of Wales a sense of being one nation.

Llywelyn became more and more powerful. King Henry III was distracted by a rebellion in England and Llywelyn made alliances with Henry's enemies. He married Eleanor, the daughter of Henry's enemy, Simon de Montfort.

In 1267, Henry recognised Llywelyn as Prince of Wales but in return Llywelyn had to pay very high tribute. He paid once but then stopped, perhaps because he just did not have enough money.

Henry III died and his son Edward I became king. Llywelyn refused to pay tribute and did not go to Edward's coronation. Edward called Llywelyn a rebel and attacked his lands in Wales.

Edward was successful against Llywelyn because he managed to cut off Llywelyn's food supply. Edward told Llywelyn that if he surrendered, he would give him land in England. However, Llywelyn was not interested in land in England. By now, the Welsh were united behind him against the English. The people throughout Wales had started to get an understanding of what it meant to be Welsh.

Unfortunately, when Llywelyn was out riding he was killed by a soldier who probably did not even know who he was. His death meant the end of Welsh resistance and in 1282, Wales became an English colony.

PRINCE EDWARD, PRINCE OF WALES

THE FIRST ENGLISH PRINCE OF WALES

Caernarfon Castle

Llywelyn the Last called himself "Prince of Wales" and Henry III had accepted that. However, when Edward became king, he called Llywelyn a rebel. The Welsh dreams of remaining independent died with

Llywelyn the Last. Llywelyn's brother Dafydd took the title but died himself just a year later.

You may know the film "Braveheart" with Mel Gibson which tells the story of William Wallace leading the Scots against the English. The English king he fights is Edward I, also known by the names "Long-shanks" (because he was very tall and had long legs) and "Hammer of the Scots". This is the same Edward who was fighting the Welsh. Even after Dafydd's death, the Welsh still rebelled and Edward had to find ways to make his power felt. However, it was difficult for him to fight both the Scots and the Welsh at the same time.

There is a legend that Edward made an agreement with the Welsh leaders. He promised he would give them a prince of Wales to replace Llywelyn. This prince, he said, would be someone who was born in Wales and could not speak English. Sometime later, Edward presented the Welsh leaders with his baby son, Edward. He had been born in Caernarfon Castle and was so young that he could not speak English. And so, Edward was made the first Prince of Wales.

The story is untrue. Edward's son was not made Prince of Wales until he was 16. However, the story shows how the Welsh felt about the English king taking over their country.

In the centuries which followed, the English monarch always gave the title to their eldest son. After Edward only one more Prince of Wales was actually born in Wales – Henry V who was born in Monmouth in 1386.

Welsh Language IV

The Mabinogion

Giants, white horses appearing from nowhere, heroic men and beautiful and clever women – these are the characters from the stories in "The Mabinogion".

The stories were first collected in two books, the "White Book of Rhydderch" (1300-1325) and the "Red Book of Hergest" (1375-1425). However, some of the stories were written down in the second half of the 11th century and many are much older and had been passed on orally through the generations.

The Mabinogi are a collection of different stories. Some are myths or legends and they are all magical.

The first myths are the original "Mabinogi", four stories about a man called Pryderi. We learn about 1) Pryderi's parents; 2) a woman called Branwen marrying the King of Ireland; 3) Pryderi and Branwen's brother coming home to Wales and 4) a conflict Pryderi has with two men called Math and Gwydion.

There are also five stories based on Welsh legends, including one about the Welsh king Macsen Wledig (the historical figure Magnus Maximus) who rebelled against the Romans. There are several stories which feature King Arthur.

The final three stories are romances, early Welsh versions of Arthurian love stories.

In the 19th century, Lady Charlotte Guest translated the tales into English and they became very popular. The stories have influenced writers throughout the ages, including, for example, J.R.R. Tolkien in his book "The Silmarillion".

Visit Wales IV

The Great Castles

When Edward I conquered Wales in 1282, he knew that he had to act to make sure the Welsh "snake lying in the grass" would not fight back. He got rid of any symbols of Llywelyn's rule, like the seals[1] of office. He

---

1. a special mark you put on an official document

replaced Hywel's law with English law and changed how the country was ruled. Taxes increased by 600% for the poorest and Edward introduced different levels of taxes for different people. For example, the English settlers paid far less than the native Welsh people.

He built castles, known as the "iron ring". He took castles built by Llywelyn the Great, like Criccieth Castle and others. He then built 17 new Norman castles. Four of the most impressive castles built by Edward I are Conwy, Caernarvon, Harlech and Beaumaris. They were built according to a special design, building "walls within walls". All of them also had access to the sea. Conwy, Caernarvon and Beaumaris had walled towns alongside them.

These four castles are now a UNESCO World Heritage site. The UN-ESCO said they are "the finest examples of late 13th and early 14th century military architecture in Europe". If you are in north Wales, a visit to these castles is a "must".

While you are in Conwy, there are two other interesting houses to visit. One is a large Elizabethan House called "**Plas Mawr**" (meaning Big Place), built for a rich merchant in the late 16th century. It is said to be the best house from this period in the UK.

Then you can go from the "Big Place", to the "Small Place"! In fact, to the smallest house in the UK! The house is less than 1.83 m wide and 3.10 m tall. In 1900, the local authorities decided it was no longer fit for anyone to live there. The last person to live in the house was a fisherman who was 1.91m tall.

According to the Guinness Book of Records, it is officially the smallest house in Britain.

THE
RENAISSANCE

Owain Glyndŵr,
Corwen,
North Wales

Pembroke Castle,
Pembrokeshire

THE RENAISSANCE

By the end of the Middle Ages, Wales was under the control of the English king. In the centuries which followed, the Welsh once again fought the English. Eventually Wales was legally joined to England and in the 16th century, the English kings and queens had ancestors[1] from Wales.

In this chapter, we meet a Welsh man who took on the English king, a mathematician, a translator and the first king of England with Welsh ancestors. The travel tips take you back to Pembrokeshire where there is so much more to discover!

King Henry VII &
Queen Elizabeth,
Cardiff Castle

---

1. ancestor = a member of your family who lived before you

Owain Glyndŵr (1349-1416)

Owain Glyndŵr was born in 1354. Both his father and his mother had royal Welsh blood. His father died when he was young and Glyndŵr went to live with a judge. He was well-educated and went to the law schools at the Inns of Court in London. Later, he married the judge's daughter and the couple had six sons and a number of daughters. Glyndŵr lived a comfortable life with his family, living close to the Welsh-English border in north Wales.

When Glyndŵr was born, Edward III was king. In 1377, Edward's grandson became King Richard II. Glyndŵr was faithful to the English king and fought in his army against the Scots. However, Richard II was not a good king and the barons were unhappy. In 1399, one of the barons, Richard's cousin Henry Bolingbroke rebelled and made himself King Henry IV. Richard was imprisoned and later murdered.

Henry IV taxed the Welsh heavily. The new king also refused to help Glyndŵr in a disagreement with his neighbour, calling the Welshman a "barefoot rascal".

Glyndŵr was angry, as were many other noble Welsh families. In 1400, Glyndŵr's 300 supporters declared him Prince of Wales. This showed the king that the Welsh still remembered Llywelyn the Last and his fight against King Edward just over a hundred years earlier. The Welsh were ready to fight again. Welsh barons, young students as well farm workers all joined to fight with Glyndŵr. They attacked English towns near the border.

Henry's army fought back, but Glyndŵr had already become a local hero and by 1401 all of north and mid Wales supported him.

Glyndŵr captured his neighbour and enemy and asked a ransom for him of £6,666. Later he captured the King's nephew Edmund Mortimer. Henry believed Mortimer was not faithful and had chosen to join Glyndŵr. Mortimer was disappointed with the king's reaction and so he did join Glyndŵr and married Catrin, Glyndŵr's daughter. Mortimer had a better claim to the English throne than Henry himself and so this was a very good alliance for Glyndŵr.

Glyndŵr took back the original Welsh castles in Wales and even took the Norman castle Harlech, built by Edward I. However, Glyndŵr's luck did not last. His castles were re-taken by the English and his wife and children were captured. By 1410, he was an outlaw. Henry offered rewards if the Welsh would hand over Glyndŵr but no-one did. He was never found and we do not know for sure when or where he died.

In Wales, he has become a mythical character like King Arthur. If Wales is in trouble, the Welsh believe that this charismatic leader will return and rescue them again.

Henry VII (1457-1509)

The Tudors - a Welsh Dynasty

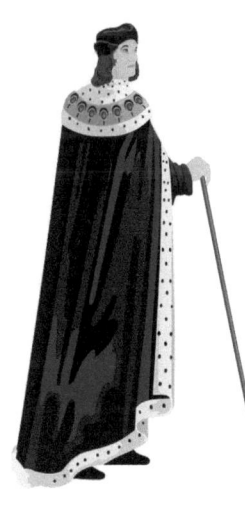

Henry IV died in 1413 and his son Henry V became king. Henry married the French princess Catherine de Vallois after fighting against the French and defeating them at Agincourt. Shakespeare writes about this famous battle in his play about Henry's life ("Henry V").

Henry and Catherine had just one son and the young king died at the age of 35. His son was a baby when he became Henry VI and his uncles, the brothers of Henry V, reigned for him until he was 16.

He was a weak king and during his reign, members of his family rebelled and started what has become known as the

War of the Roses where the York and Lancaster families fought for the crown.

Henry's mother, Catherine, who was only 20 when her husband died, caused a great scandal by falling in love with a servant at court. This, at least, is the English version of the story. The "servant" at court was in fact a Welsh nobleman called Owen Tudor. Owen's father and uncles were related to and fought with Owain Glyndŵr.

Owen and Queen Catherine had three sons. Owen and his two eldest sons, Edmund and Jasper supported their Lancastrian half-brother Henry VI in the War of the Roses. Owen was executed[1] after one of the battles against the Yorkist army. Henry rewarded Owen's sons and gave them titles. They held important positions which no Welshman had ever held before.

In 1455, Edmund married Margaret Beaufort. She was the great-great-granddaughter of Edward III and had a claim to the throne. She was only 12 years old when they married ... and he was her second "husband". Her first "husband" died before they were lived together and Margaret never counted it as a real marriage. It was normal for the daughters of noble families to be married at very young ages but it was also normal that a husband wait until his wife was old enough before sleeping with her. Twenty-four-year-old Edmund, however, did not wait.

Edmund was captured a year later during fighting with the Yorkist army and died of plague[2] in prison, leaving his 13-year-old wife Mar-

---

1. execute = to kill someone as punishment for a crime

2. plague = a very serious disease which killed millions of people in the Middle Ages

garet, who was already seven months pregnant. After a difficult birth, Henry Tudor was born in Pembroke Castle. Margaret's brother-in-law Jasper, made sure that Margaret remarried so that she would be safe. He looked after Henry and the two of them fled to Brittany for the reign of the Yorkist king Edward IV.

While Henry was in France, King Edward died and his brother Richard became king. At the beginning of August 1485, Henry arrived back in south Wales with his uncle Jasper and about 2,000 French soldiers. He soon gathered support from the Welsh and on 22nd August, his army fought King Richard III's on Bosworth Field. Henry won partly because his mother's third husband changed sides to help Henry during the battle. Henry Tudor became King Henry VII and married King Edward IV's daughter Elizabeth as a sign that the war between the houses of York (with the symbol of a white rose) and Lancaster (red rose) had ended. The Tudor rose is a red and white rose combined.

The couple had three sons and four daughters. Three children survived – including King Henry VIII of England, famous for his six wives, Margaret who became Queen of Scotland and Mary who became Queen of France.

Henry VII reigned for 24 years and died in 1509. He was the first king of England who had Welsh ancestors.

ROBERT RECORDE (1512-1558)

Can you imagine maths without the mathematical signs?

+ plus
- minus
× multiply
÷ divide
= equals

But do you know where the signs come from?

With a slightly different meaning, the plus and minus signs were being used in Germany in the late 15th century by mathematician Johannes Widmann. They were introduced to Britain in the late 16th century by the Welsh mathematician, Robert Recorde.

Recorde was born in Tenby, in south-west Wales in around 1512. He studied at both Oxford and Cambridge universities and became a medical doctor. He was doctor to both King Edward VI and later Queen Mary I (both grandchildren of Henry VII). He was also the controller of the Royal Mint which made the money for England and Wales.

He wrote a number of books about medicine and mathematics. In one published in 1557, he introduced the equals sign (=).

Unfortunately, Recorde made some powerful enemies in his political roles and he died in a debtors' prison in 1558. There is a plaque in the church in Tenby in memory of Recorde.

St Mary's Church, Tenby

Welsh Language V

The Welsh Bible

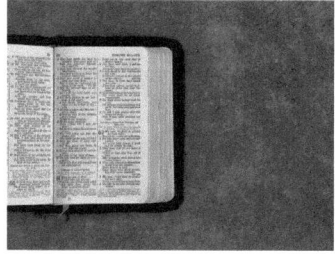

After Henry VIII split from the Roman Church, religious life in Britain became complicated. Henry's church had not experienced a religious reformation. Henry hated Reformers like Luther and Calvin. Henry just needed a church without the Pope as its head.

His son Edward VI was a protestant with more reformed ideas, but when he died and his sister Queen Mary I became queen, she re-introduced Roman Catholicism. She persecuted protestants which led to her being given the name "Bloody Mary". However, Mary only reigned for five years and when her sister Elizabeth became queen, the country changed back to Protestantism.

Many people in England and Wales were not happy about this and worshipped in the Catholic way in secret. Elizabeth realised that it would be good if the people of Wales could go to the official church and hear the Bible read in their own language. In 1563, parliament ordered the Welsh bishops to make Welsh translations of the Bible and the Prayer Book used in the church.

William Salesbury and a team of academics translated the New Testament into Welsh and it was published in 1567.

William Morgan, another Welsh scholar, was very happy that the New Testament was available in Welsh but believed that the Old Testament should also be translated. In the 1580s he began working on a translation. His Old Testament and Salesbury's New Testament were published together for the first time in 1588.

The translation is extremely important in the history and development of the Welsh language. At the time, most people in Wales spoke only Welsh. In 1536, England and Wales had been officially joined under king Henry VIII. Wales now had the same religion and the same laws as in England. At the same time, the official legal language became English. As a Welsh speaker, it was possible to be arrested, tried and executed in Wales without understanding a word. Having the Bible translated into Welsh, gave the language more status.

The Welsh people were the thirteenth nation who were able to read the Bible in their native language. This translation is still used today.

VISIT WALES V

BACK TO PEMBROKESHIRE

Pembrokeshire is a very popular place to visit. As well as following in the steps of the Welsh saints, there is so much more to see.

There are many castles in Pembrokeshire. **Carew Castle** was the castle where the Welsh princess Nest lived with her husband Gerald of Windsor. This is the castle Owain attacked and set on fire so that he could kidnap her.

The castle where Henry Tudor was born is also well worth a visit. There has been a castle in **Pembroke** since the 11th century but most of the castle we see today was built in the 12th century.

In **Tenby**, brighritly coloured houses line the streets and, as well as a busy town centre with shops, the town has two big sandy beaches. If you can tear yourself away from the beach, there is plenty to do and see. You can visit Tenby's main church, St Mary's and see the monument to Robert Recorde, take a walk around the castle mound or visit the Tudor Merchant's House. Tenby was an important port in the Middle Ages and items imported included linen[1], salt, sugar, and wine. In the house, you can see how a merchant lived in the Tudor period.

If you like an outdoor holiday, Pembrokeshire is an excellent place to try "coasteering". This activity includes swimming in the sea, jumping off cliffs and discovering caves. You can find out more here https://coasteering.co.uk/what-is-coasteering/. If this seems a little too adventurous, why not go for a walk instead. The part of the Welsh coastal path which goes through Pembrokeshire is especially beautiful.

---

1. linen = a light cloth made from flax

INDUSTRIALISATION
& SOCIAL REFORM

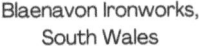
Coalworks

Blaenavon Ironworks,
South Wales

INDUSTRIALISATION AND SOCIAL REFORM

In the early 18th century, Wrexham and Carmarthen were the biggest towns in Wales with around 2,000 people each. Most people at the time still worked on farms. However, the 18th and 19th centuries would bring many changes to Britain and the rest of the world.

New discoveries and inventions brought huge developments in technology. Wales had many of the resources needed for the new industries. **Copper** was rediscovered in north Wales by a man called Rowland Pugh. Pugh was rewarded for his find. He was given a bottle of whisky and a cottage to live in rent-free for the rest of his life. The local lawyer Thomas Williams, on the other hand, gained control of the Parys Mine Company. Within twelve years he was "Copper King" and Parys was the biggest copper mine in Europe. His main customer was the British Navy who needed copper for their ships. The copper stopped shellfish growing on the bottom of the ship and so made the ships faster.

Wales also had **lead**, as well as **iron, slate** and **coal**. Coal was found in the valleys in south Wales and as three tons of coal was needed to smelt one ton of copper, the copper was transported to the town of Swansea on the south coast. Swansea had everything. The coal fields were nearby and coal could be transported down the river to the copper works. Water from the river was used for cooling and Swansea also had a big harbour to ship the copper when it was ready. Swansea became "Copperopolis" and copper was brought from as far away as north and south America to be smelt in Swansea. By 1820, half of the global copper industry was based in Swansea.

Wales was the first industrialised country on the planet[1] and industrialisation made winners and losers. The new technologies made some people, like Thomas Williams extremely rich. However, it also brought great suffering to the workers who lived in poverty. Swansea was the first industrial site in Wales. The gases were poisonous, people died young and acid rain killed plants and animals. Poverty and terrible conditions brought revolutions and social reforms in the 18th and 19th centuries.

Wales was at the heart of both technology and social unrest during this period. In this chapter, prepare to meet pirates, entrepreneurs, revolutionaries, and poets and see how a new feeling of "Welshness" was created both in Wales and amongst the Welsh in England.

The travel tips for this chapter take you to the south Wales valleys, where you can learn about heavy industry, enjoy beautiful landscape and buy a book or two in the book capital of the world.

---

1. A country is industrialised when more people are involved in industry than in farming. Wales was the first country in the world where this was the case.

Dic Penderyn

The Merthyr Rising 1808-1831

 While Swansea became "Copperopolis", the centre of the global copper trade, Merthyr Tydfil was to become home to the largest and most profitable ironworks in the world.

In 1760, Merthyr Tydfil was a small farming village and was home to about 40 people. However, this tiny place had everything needed for the iron industry: iron ore, coal and fast flowing water in the streams and the River Taff. One hundred years later, Merthyr was the biggest town in Wales. 50,000 people lived and worked here under extremely difficult conditions.

While the owners of the ironworks became rich and built luxurious homes like the Crawshay family's Cafarthfa Castle, many of the workers and their families lived in slums. In Merthyr, 1,500 people lived in family units in tiny huts (1.2m by 2.1m) which were built on the rubbish from the ironworks. There were no toilets and no clean water. Illnesses were common and if cholera began in the slums, it could kill whole families within hours. In 1849, 1,800 people died of cholera in Merthyr alone.

In May 1831, the workers started a protest. Workers in other towns joined the movement and in June, 10,000 people marched into Merthyr demanding cheaper bread and higher wages. The ironwork owners refused and called in the army to restore order. The people took rags and dipped them into cow's blood and then tied them to sticks. It was the first time that a red flag was used as a symbol of workers' rights.

The army opened fire on the crowd and many were injured and some killed. However, they could not control the crowd. The magistrates and owners of the ironworks hid in the hotel for a week but then finally, the crowds went away and the army took back control.

Twenty-four people died and twenty-six were arrested. Most of those arrested were sent to a penal colony in Australia but one young man, a miner called Richard Lewis was condemned for attacking a soldier. 11,000 people signed a petition asking for Lewis to be released but the English government wanted to make an example of someone. Richard Lewis, who is known as Dic Penderyn, was just 23 years old when he was hanged in Cardiff in August 1831.

Dic Penderyn's death made people very angry and strengthened the trade union movement. It also encouraged calls for working men to be given a democratic voice. This movement was called Chartism.

ROBERT OWEN (1771-1858)

ENTREPRENEUR AND SOCIAL REFORMER

Robert Owen.

Most entrepreneurs in this period treated their workers as badly as Crayshaw. However, there were some exceptions.

Robert Owen was born in 1771 and did not go to school, although he did love reading. He started working in his hometown of Newtown in Wales at the age of nine. At ten, he moved to England to learn about the cloth trade. He worked selling cloth in London and then moved to Manchester, centre of the cloth trade at the time, and started making spinning machines. He worked as a manager of different cotton mills in Manchester and was sent on a business trip to Glasgow. Owen got on well with the millowner David Dale, who shared his philosophical ideas. Owen also fell in love with Dale's daughter and they got married.

In 1799, Owen bought his father-in-law's mill in New Lanark in Scotland. 2,000 people worked at the mill and 500 of them were children from poorhouses in Glasgow and Edinburgh who started working at the mill aged five or six. The workers lived in very poor conditions.

Owen wanted to test his social and economic ideas at his new mill. Could he make life better for his workers and still make a profit? He began to offer free education to the children and they did not begin work until they were over 10 years old. He also offered free childcare so that mothers could go back to work.

At the time, it was usual for workers to be paid with special tokens instead of money. That way, the workers could only spend the tokens in the shops which belonged to the millowner. The goods sold there were expensive but of low quality. In Owen's shops, however, the workers could buy good quality goods which were only a little more than the wholesale price Owen had paid for them. These shops are the basis for the co-operative shops which still function today.

Owen campaigned for an eight-hour working day. His slogan was "eight hours labour (work), eight hours recreation, eight hours rest". The workers in his own mill only worked eight hours a day. Owen believed that if he could show that his ideas were better than the capitalist system, others would also start to live in the same way. Owen showed that it was possible to treat workers well and still make a good profit.

Owen and his sons started similar communities in the United States and had meetings with many important politicians of the time to explain his ideas. He even gave a speech to Congress in the House of Representatives. Unfortunately, his model community in Pennsylvania failed and Owen lost a lot of his money.

Owen moved to London and gave up his mill in Scotland. He continued to promote free education and better living conditions for workers in factory towns. He was involved in the early trade unions. Engels and Marx admired his ideas, although they believed that radical social change would only happen if capitalism was overthrown by force.

Owen returned to Wales at the end of his life and died there in 1858, aged 87. Owen's ideas were well ahead of his time and he has been called the "Father of British Socialism".

"REBECCA!"

It was not only the workers in urban Wales who protested against injustice. On the night of 13th May 1839, a group of men dressed as women and with blackened faces attacked a tollgate and tollhouse near Efailwen, in Carmarthenshire in south Wales. They returned every night for a week until the tollgate and tollhouse were completely destroyed. The protest went on for three years and 200 tollgates were attacked as well as workhouses and other buildings. The movement became known as the **Rebecca Riots**.

Roads through the countryside were controlled by private companies called Turnpike Trusts. They charged people to use the roads. In Wales especially, the farmers were angry. They had to pay the landowners so that they could farm the land. They had to pay church tax to the

Church of England although they went to the independent chapels. They had to pay taxes for the workhouses they hated and finally they had to pay a road tax to take their produce to markets. They could not survive on what was left after they had paid all these taxes and in 1839, the decided to fight back.

As soon as the tollgate in Carmarthenshire was rebuilt, they attacked it for a second time. This time shouting, "Rebecca!"

It is believed that the deeply religious people named their movement after a verse in their bibles. In Genesis, it says of Rebecca, "And they blessed Rebecca and said to her, 'Our sister, may you become the mother of many, and **may your children take the gates of your enemies**'."[1]

The protesters had support throughout society, even from some of the landowners. In autumn 1843, the government agreed with the protesters and introduced laws to stop the Turnpike Trusts charging such high tolls for using the roads. This time at least, the people had won.

---

1. Genesis 24 v 60

JOHN FROST (1784-1877) & GEORGE SHELL (1820-1839)

THE NEWPORT UPRISING

In 19th century Britain, fewer than 5% of the population were allowed to vote. In the 1830s, more and more working-class men began to demand the right to vote. In 1838, the People's Charter was drawn up in London. Among other things, it called for votes for all men over 21 and for voting to be done in secret ballots.

The Chartists who wrote the Charter wanted immediate change but parliament refused to even debate it. A Cardiff tailor called John Frost and some other Chartist leaders, planned to march to the town of Newport, demanding change. On 3 November 1839, 20,000 protesters set off on the march. One of them was a 19-year-old man called George Shell. Shell wrote to his parents the night before the protest, telling them that he was taking part in "a struggle for freedom" and he was willing to die for the cause.

The Welsh weather was against the protesters on that day. Because of the rain, many protesters never made it to the place they had agreed to meet. Others waited in the rain and set off late. By the time they finally got to Newport, the 5,000 marchers who did make it were wet, cold and exhausted.

The government had sent soldiers to stop the protesters. A shot was fired. Some said the soldiers fired first, while others said one of the protestors fired their gun by mistake. After the shot, there was a 25-minute battle. At the end of it, 20 protestors were dead and many wounded. George Shell was the youngest victim. The dead protestors were buried at night in unmarked graves.

200 protestors were arrested, including John Frost. He and two other organisers were found guilty of treason which meant they were sentenced to death. The public was shocked and called for justice and the men were spared. Instead, they were sent to Tasmania.

After 14 years, Frost was pardoned under the condition that he did not return to Britain. He went to America with his daughter. Two years later, he received an unconditional pardon and returned to the UK.

Chartism was never successful in creating reforms. Its ideas were seen as too extreme. However, some reforms were made in the 1860s, secret voting was introduced in 1872 and all men over the age of 21 finally got the vote in 1918.

After returning to Britain, Frost continued to support reform and social justice. He died in Bristol in 1877, aged 93.

Bartholomew Roberts (1682-1722)

The most successful Pirate

Bartholomew Roberts was born in a sleepy village in Pembrokeshire in 1682. At the age of 13, he went to sea and served on a number of ships. In 1719, he was serving on a slave ship when it was attacked by pirates.

At first, he did not want to become a pirate, but he soon saw that one could become very rich as a pirate. It may have helped that the captain of the two pirate ships was also a Welshman called Davis. Davis saw that Roberts was a good navigator and he began to tell Roberts secrets in Welsh so that the other sailors could not understand.

Just six weeks after Roberts had joined the pirates, Davis was shot on the island of Principe and Roberts was chosen as the new captain.

Roberts took revenge for the death of Davis, killing many of the men who lived on Principe and taking whatever they could carry. He then took a Dutch ship and two days later a British navy ship.

He asked the crew where they wanted to go next and they chose Brazil. While they were there, they captured a Portuguese ship carrying 40,000 gold coins and jewellery for the King of Portugal. Roberts then took one of the ships and some of the men to go after another ship. When they returned, they found that one of the pirates had made himself captain and left with the stolen goods.

Roberts decided that the crew needed rules about how to behave. They wrote a pirate's code and the crew members swore on the bible that they would live by the code. The code meant that all decisions were made democratically and all the sailors got the same share of whatever they took. Gambling was forbidden and they had to turn their lights out at 8 o'clock in the evening. Fighting on board the ship and smuggling women on board was strictly forbidden. Drinking was allowed but Roberts himself was teetotal (meaning he did not drink alcohol).

Roberts died fighting a Royal Navy ship. When they saw that he was dead, his crew wrapped his body in the sail, weighed it down and threw it overboard, as he had always said he wanted to be buried at sea.

In his four-year career, Roberts captured over 400 ships. He was the most successful pirate of the so-called Golden Age of Piracy (1650-1730).

IOLO MORGANWG (1747-1826)

CREATOR OF WELSH LEGEND

Every summer, the **Eisteddfod** is held in Wales. The word "Eisteddfod" comes from the Welsh "to sit" and is a celebration of Welsh culture with poetry, music and dancing. It is believed that the first Eisteddfod was held in 1176. However, the Eisteddfod traditions we see today have their roots in the late 18th century.

In the 18th century, travelling schools were set up to teach people to read so that they could read the bible in Welsh. They were extremely successful and Catherine the Great, Empress of Russia, sent officials to Wales to find out more about how the schools worked. As more and more people learned to read, more and more books were produced. However, Wales itself had no cultural or intellectual centres. There were no universities in Wales. If a clever Welsh person wanted a good education, they had to leave Wales and go to England. This is the reason that many clever young men from Wales found themselves in London where they formed Welsh-speaking groups.

One such young man was Edward Williams. Williams was a talented poet. As a poet, or bard, he called himself Iolo Morganwg. After visiting Stonehenge, Williams became more and more interested in ancient British customs. As he could find very few texts about the Druids who he believed lived in this period, he decided to create his own! Probably helped by his use of laudanum[1], he wrote a collection of 'medieval' poetry which he said were ancient texts that he had found.

In 1791, he created the **Gorsedd**, a meeting of Welsh poets who met according to "ancient" Druidic rites which had in fact been invented by Williams. The Gorsedd is now a part of the Eisteddfod which has been held every year (except 1914 and 1940) since its revival in 1880. The word Gorsedd comes from the Welsh word for "throne" and the winner of the poetry award is still crowned on a throne today.

Williams was part of the "Celtic Revival", an interest in ancient traditions in Wales and Scotland. It was not until the end of the 19th century, long after Williams's death, that people realised that many of the 'ancient' manuscripts which he had 'discovered' had in fact been written by Williams himself.

Even though the ideas of Welshness were created in Edward Williams's imagination and with the help of drugs, they were very important in developing a Welsh identity and remembering a romantic past before industrialisation destroyed the countryside of Williams's south Wales valleys.

---

1. a drug made from opium

WELSH LANGUAGE VI

THE NATIONAL ANTHEM

If you have ever seen a rugby match where Wales is playing, you will have heard the national anthem sung with great passion by the team and all the spectators! It has an emotional text set to a rousing tune.

It was written in 1856 by Evan James who wrote the text and James James, his son who wrote the music. It was very popular when it was sung in their home town of Maesteg in south Wales, as it was two years later when it was sung at the Eisteddfod. It expressed the growing national feeling of the people.

The Welsh national anthem was the first one to be sung at a sporting event. The New Zealand rugby team begin each match with a haka[1]

---

1. If you have never seen a haka, you can see one here
   https://www.youtube.com/watch?v=yiKFYTFJ_kw.
   It has to be seen to be believed!

and in response, in 1905, one of the Welsh players led the crowd in singing the anthem.

The song is not the official anthem but it is sung on many official and unofficial occasions. Below is the text in Welsh and a translation in English.[2]

Mae hen wlad fy nhadau yn annwyl i mi,
Gwlad beirdd a chantorion, enwogion o fri;
Ei gwrol ryfelwyr, gwladgarwyr tra mâd,
Tros ryddid gollasant eu gwaed.

Gwlad! Gwlad! Pleidiol wyf i'm gwlad.
Tra môr yn fur i'r bur hoff bau,
O bydded i'r hen iaith barhau.

The old land of my fathers is dear to me,
Land of bards and singers,
famous men of renown;
Her brave warriors, very splendid patriots,
For freedom shed their blood.

Country, Country, I am faithful to my Country.
While the sea [is] a wall to the pure, most loved land,
O may the old language endure.

---

2. You can see the rugby team singing the anthem here
https://www.youtube.com/watch?v=aVZHklqNGoo

Visit Wales VI

The South Wales Valleys

The south Wales valleys combine stunning countryside with sites from Wales's industrial past. On a visit to the **Big Pit National Coal Museum**, you can travel deep down into the coal mine in Blaenafon and find out what life was like for the men and boys who worked down in the darkness.[1]

To see how the other half lived, you can visit **Cafarthfa Castle** in Merthyr. It was the home of the rich owner of the Merthyr ironworks, William Crawshay II who built the mansion in 1824. As well as walking around the museum in the main house, you can enjoy the beautiful park with the lake or take a ride on the miniature steam train.

The **Brecon Beacons**, or in Welsh Bannau Brycheiniog, are the highest mountains in south Wales. From the highest of the peaks, Pen y Fan, you can see all the way down to the sea on a clear day. The area is a National Park and, as well as hiking, there are lots of things to do, including cycling, horse riding, rock climbing and fishing.

In the Brecon Beacons, you can also find one of four Welsh whisky distilleries. Penderyn Distillery offers tours and you can pick up a bottle of fine Welsh whisky.

Another wonderful place to visit in the Brecon Beacons is **Hay-on-Wye**. This pretty little town on the River Wye is half in Wales and half in England. 1,500 people live in this sleepy little place with its medieval castle. However, the town is famous for one reason only – its bookshops! Hay-on-Wye has over twenty bookshops. The shops sell both new and second-hand books. There are special bookshops for children's books or murder mystery books. Some sell valuable antiquarian books and in others you can pick up a paperback for under a pound. In May and June, there is a Book Festival which attracts writers and booklovers from all over the world. Bill Clinton once called it "The Woodstock of the mind".

---

1. For more information, see https://museum.wales/bigpit/

MODERN WALES

Cardiff Bay

Swansea Marina

MODERN WALES

At the beginning of the 20th century, coal was still in high demand and in 1913, the industry employed 250,000 men. However, after the Second World War, the demand for coal began to decline. In the 60s, 75,000 men worked in the industry and by 1979, 30,000. 1966 saw one of the worst disasters in Wales's history, when a tip of waste from the mine slipped down the mountain and into the village of Aberfan. It covered the primary school and 109 children and 5 teachers were killed.

The coal industry continued to dominate life in Wales into the 1980s when Margaret Thatcher's government refused to meet the demands of the miners and they went on strike.

In the 20th century, the population of Wales increased from just over 2 million to 2.9 million. As most of the new people came from out-side Wales, English became the dominant language, especially in the south Wales valleys. The fate of the language was once again linked to the political situation. *Plaid Cymru*, a left-wing nationalist party was formed in 1925. They won their first seat in the UK parliament in 1966.

But still, by the 1980s, many feared that the Welsh language would die out.

In this chapter, we will look at two important Welsh politicians who both left a legacy which continues today, an inspirational teacher, the trouble around Charles's investiture as Prince of Wales and how the people of Wales finally got the power to make their own decisions.

In our travel tips, we will find out what you can see in Wales's capital city, Cardiff.

DAVID LLOYD GEORGE (1863-1945)

PRIME MINISTER (1916-1922)

Winston Churchill described David Lloyd George as the greatest political genius of the day who had more political insight than any other statesman.

David George was born in Manchester to Welsh parents. His father was ill and unfortunately, he died before David's first birthday. As a result, David's mother took her family to live with her brother in a small village in North Wales. Her brother, Richard Lloyd was a shoemaker, as well as a church minister and a strong supporter of the Liberal Party. He had a great influence on David and encouraged him to study law and later to enter politics. David loved his uncle and took his name to became David Lloyd George.

David went to the village Anglican school, where he had to speak English, but at home his first language was Welsh.

He set up his own firm as a solicitor[1] and he was very successful. He was able to hire his brother in the firm and opened offices in a number of towns in the area. He was always interested in politics and in 1890, he became an MP (Member of Parliament) for Caernarfon. He would serve as their MP in the British parliament for 55 years.

The young MP was the first Welsh politician to support the idea that Wales should have powers to make its own decisions (devolution). He supported the establishment of the National Library of Wales, as well as the National Museum of Wales.

In 1908, Lloyd George became Chancellor of the Exchequer, responsible for finances in the British government. He introduced major social reforms, including new taxes and payments for those who were too ill to work. It was the beginning of the welfare state in Britain. During his time as Prime Minister (1916-1922), many other reforms were introduced, including minimum wages for farmers and payments for workers who lost their jobs. Children had to go to school until the age of 14 and it became illegal for children under 14 to work. Pensions were doubled and immigrants who had lived and worked in Britain for more than ten years could claim the same pensions as British-born workers.

---

1. a solicitor is a lawyer who prepares documents and gives advice on legal matters

Under Lloyd George, there was also a reform of the voting system. Men were given the vote as well as most women over 30.

Lloyd George negotiated the terms of the end of the First World War. He wanted Germany to pay reparations but did not want to completely destroy the German economy.

In 1921, he had to negotiate again. This time in Ireland. There had been troubles and fighting in Ireland where many people wanted Ireland to become independent. As a result of these talks, the southern part of Ireland became the Irish Free State, while in the north, a part of the island which wanted to stay part of the United Kingdom, became what we know as Northern Ireland.

Lloyd George died of cancer, aged 82 in March 1945. He is believed to be one of the most important Prime Ministers of modern times.

Aneurin Bevan (1897-1960)

Father of the NHS

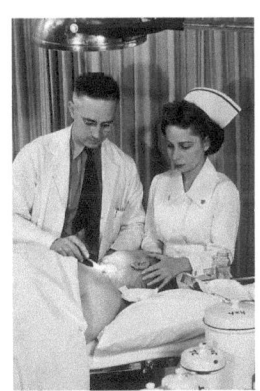

"I do not represent the big bosses at the top. I represent the people at the bottom [...]"
Aneurin Bevan, 1944

Aneurin Bevan was born in 1897 in Tredegar in the South Wales valleys. His family was poor and Bevan left school at 13 to work in the local coal mine alongside his father and older brother. He became involved with the trade union and spent all his free time reading in the local library.

In 1919, he received a scholarship to go to London to study economics, history and politics. When he returned to Wales, he became a leading figure in the union movement and one of the leaders of the miners in the General Strike of 1926.

Bevan became involved in local politics and in 1929, he became a Member of Parliament. It was in the Houses of Parliament that he met his wife, Jennie Lee who was a Scottish MP.

In 1945, after the War, the Labour Party won the General Election for the first time[1]. Bevan was asked to join the Cabinet as Minister for Health and Housing. He was responsible for building houses (over a million were built before 1950) and for his greatest achievement – the creation of the National Health Service (NHS) in 1948. It was based on a system which Bevan knew from his home town of Tredegar. There, people paid a small fee and could then receive medical and dental care when they needed it.

The NHS was paid for by taxes and anyone who needed medical care could receive it "free at the point of use".

Labour won the next General Election in 1950 and Bevan was made Minister for Labour but he did not keep the job for long. When the NHS was introduced, many people who could not afford to see a doctor before, now used the new health service. It was being overwhelmed

---

1. The Labour Party had formed governments before (in 1924 and 1929) but 1945 was the first time they had won a majority.

and in 1952, a fee was introduced for prescriptions. Bevan believed this was wrong and resigned from the cabinet.

Later the same year, Labour lost the election and Bevan never had the chance to be part of a government again. He was still active in parliament, though and remained an MP until his death of stomach cancer in 1960. Two days after his death, Harold Macmillan, the Conservative Prime Minister called Aneurin Bevan, "a great personality and a great national figure".

He will always be remembered for being the father of the NHS. Health systems all over the world are struggling with ageing societies and the aftermath of the Covid 19 pandemic. A lack of government funding even before the pandemic has led to big problems for the NHS – for example, not enough workers, old and crumbling hospitals, long waiting lists to see a doctor, receive a diagnosis or have an operation. However, in a comparison of healthcare systems, the NHS still surprisingly performs better than other European countries, including France, Germany and Switzerland.[2]

In 2014, a survey found that the thing British people are most proud of, is the National Health Service. Even though everyone in the UK knows someone who cannot get the care they need from the NHS, in 2022, 90% of the population said they believed the service should be free and available to all.

---

2. https://www.commonwealthfund.org/publications/fund-report s/2021/aug/mirror-mirror-2021-reflecting-poorly#rank

Charles, Prince of Wales

Investiture and protests in 1969

"I, Charles, Prince of Wales, do become your liege man of life and limb and of earthly worship and faith and truth I will bear unto thee to live and die against all manner of folks."

This was the oath which Prince Charles swore to his mother Queen Elizabeth on 1st July 1969 at his investiture as Prince of Wales. Charles had had the title of Prince of Wales since he was nine years old, but 12 years later the special ceremony was held in Caernarfon Castle in north Wales. 19 million people watched the ceremony on the television in the United Kingdom and 500 million more around the world.

Although the ceremony seemed very old and traditional, it was only the second time that there had been such an investiture of the Prince of Wales.

The first was held in Caernarfon in 1911. King George V made his eldest son Edward[1] Prince of Wales. Charles's investiture was similar but his uncle, Lord Snowdon, Princess Margaret's husband, made the ceremony look more modern and suitable for the TV.

At the time of Charles's investiture, 75% of people in Wales thought it was a good idea, although 50% of the population worried that it was too expensive. However, some people were unhappy about the ceremony and about the rule of the English in Wales in general. Several things had happened which made some Welsh people feel that the English did not really care about what happened in Wales.

One such event happened in 1965. In the 1950s, the English city of Liverpool built hundreds of houses so that people could move out of the slums in the inner city. These new houses needed more and more water. They already got their water from Wales but it was decided that a valley in north Wales should be flooded to provide a new reservoir for Liverpool and the nearby area, the Wirral. There was a Welsh-speaking village in the valley but the council in Liverpool did not care about that. The houses and farms of the 75 inhabitants of Capel Celyn would be flooded, as well as their chapel, school and post office. The people of Wales fought against the plan for nine years but the city of Liverpool took the matter straight to the government in Westminster, meaning that they did not need the planning permission from the local Welsh

---

1. Later Edward VIII, who reigned only briefly and then abdicated because he wanted to marry the divorced American, Wallis Simpson.

councils. In parliament, the vote passed although none of the 36 Welsh MPs voted in favour of it. In 1965, Capel Celyn and the whole valley was flooded. The fact that the Welsh people had no political way of influencing what happened in their own country made a lot of people very angry. They wondered whether they would have to use more violent ways to get their voices heard.

The Free Wales Army, which had links to the IRA in Northern Ireland and Basque separatists in Spain, protested at the opening of the reservoir and began planting bombs. The two leaders were arrested and their trial finished on the day of the investiture. However, they were not the only such group.

Another group called MAC (meaning "Movement for the Defence of Wales") also bombed infrastructure linked to the water supply. In the following years, they began bombing political targets, too, including a site close to a building in Cardiff where Lord Snowdon was coming to discuss the investiture of the Prince of Wales. It was clear that the Welsh nationalists' anger was also aimed at the royal family and the police began to worry that there may be an attack on the day of the investiture.

In June 1969, two activists planted a bomb near the train track where the royal train would come along. The bomb exploded as they were laying it and the two men died. Two more bombs were planted in Caernarfon for the day of the investiture. One exploded in a local policeman's garden but the second one did not go off. It was found a few days later by a 10-year-old boy who was seriously hurt by the explosion.

As we will see, anger at the English would continue in the decades to come and some people were willing to use violence to show how they felt.

Despite the protests, most of the Welsh population celebrated the investiture and liked the fact that Charles wanted to do good for the nation of Wales.

In 2022, when Charles became King Charles III, Wales got their 23rd English Prince of Wales, William. A poll in the same year found that now less than half of the population (only 46%) supported the title being continued, and very few wanted to see an investiture like Charles's. It is a question which will no doubt continue to be discussed in the coming years.

BETTY CAMPBELL (1934-2017)

In September 2022, a new statue was unveiled in the centre of Cardiff. It is only the second statue of a historical woman in Cardiff. It is a statue of Betty Campbell, a woman who lived her whole life and worked in the city. So, who is she and why was a statue made of her?

Rachel Elizabeth Johnson was born in 1934 in Cardiff's Butetown, one of the UK's first multi-cultural communities. Her mother's family had come from Barbados and her father came from Jamaica. Her father was killed during the war and her mother was poor and struggled to bring up her little girl. However, Betty was very clever and won a scholarship to go to a high school for girls in Cardiff.

From a very young age, Betty wanted to be a teacher. Her teachers believed this was impossible for a black girl from a working-class background but Betty was determined.

While she was still at school, Betty became pregnant. She left and married Rupert Campbell. The couple had four children.

In 1960, Betty heard that the teacher training college in Cardiff had started to take on women. She applied and was one of only six women to be accepted. Betty studied hard and qualified as a teacher.

Betty became interested in black activists like Harriet Tubman and began to teach about black history, slavery and apartheid in South Africa. She believed it was important that the children learned about these topics.

She experienced a lot of racism but in the 1970s, she became Wales's first black headteacher.

During her life, Betty Campbell had a number of political roles and advised on matters of education and racial equality. When she died in 2017, politicians paid tribute to her and hundreds of people lined the streets of Cardiff to pay their respects.

The statue of her shows Betty Campbell surrounded by children like those she wanted to teach and inspire for the future.

THE ROAD TO DEVOLUTION

In 1979, the people of Wales voted in a referendum on the devolution of some powers to Wales. 79.7% voted against the creation of a Welsh parliament.

In 1997, the same question was asked again. This time 50.3% voted in favour of creating a Welsh parliament. It was a slim majority. But it was a majority and the Welsh parliament was created. What happened between 1979 and 1997 to change the attitudes of the Welsh people?

In 1979, Margaret Thatcher led the Conservative Party to victory in the General Election. It was the best result for the Conservatives in Wales for over a hundred years. However, the relationship to the new British government soon soured. Despite promising a Welsh language television channel, it looked as if the government would not keep their word. Only when a Welsh politician said he would go on hunger strike, did the British government create S4C, the Welsh language TV channel in 1982.

Another thing which annoyed the Welsh was that Margaret Thatcher chose English MPs to be the Secretary of State for Wales. It seemed that she wanted to give jobs to people who would support her in the cabinet, rather than people interested in Wales.

However, it was Thatcher's decision to fight the unions in the 1980s which really set the Welsh people against the Conservatives and the government in Westminster. The Miners' Strike from 1984 to 1985 was not supported by all Welsh miners. However, when all the mines closed afterwards, it left many communities without any work. The mine was the only employer in the area. Even today, parts of the south Wales valleys are some of the poorest regions in Europe.

Unemployment was high throughout the UK and not only in Wales, of course. However, Thatcher's politics made some people very rich and these people had money to spend. Many of these rich (often English) people decided to invest their money in houses in pretty parts of the country where they could spend their weekends and holidays. As more and more English people bought houses in the Welsh countryside, the prices rose and local Welsh people could no longer afford to buy houses in their own villages. This made people angry and a group called the "Sons of Glyndŵr"[1] started setting fire to the second homes of English people. Between 1979 and 1994, 220 homes were targeted and letter bombs were sent to English politicians. Naturally, not everyone agreed with the actions taken by the Sons of Glyndŵr, but many were angry about the social and political change in Wales.

The discontent had been building over hundreds of years. In the 1960s, the Welsh saw it in the flooding of Capel Celyn and the accident at Aberfan (the Coal Board was run by the English). In the 1980s, the feeling only grew and more and more people began to think that the

---

1. in memory of Owain Glyndŵr, the last Welsh Prince of Wales

Welsh needed more political power to fight against decisions made in England.

In the General Election in 1997, the Conservatives did not win a single seat in Wales.

All of these developments led to the decision in favour of devolution in 1997. While Scotland was given the power to make its own laws, Wales was originally only given the power to make decisions in certain areas, including farming, education, housing and transport.

The "National Assembly for Wales" met for the first time in May 1999. It had 60 representatives of which 24 were women. It was the first parliament in the world to have such a high proportion of representatives who were women.

In 2011, another referendum was held to find out whether the Welsh people wanted the Assembly to have law-making powers, more like the parliament in Scotland. Nearly two thirds answered "yes".

In 2020, the Assembly changed its name to "Senedd Cymru" or in English, the Welsh Parliament. Voting for the Welsh Parliament happens by proportional representation (unlike the elections for the UK parliament) and anyone over 16, as well as foreign nationals who have the right to live in Wales can vote.

WELSH LANGUAGE VII

SURVIVAL OF THE LANGUAGE

The longest place name in Wales

In 1850, 90% of the population of Wales spoke Welsh. In 1847, a report of Welsh schools was made by a group of English priests. They came to the conclusion that the main reason that Wales was not as well developed as England was due to the Welsh language. In the years that followed, children were taught in English and children who spoke Welsh in school had a piece of wood hung around their neck. This "Welsh not" was to shame the children and teach them that Welsh was forbidden. The children were often hit for speaking Welsh, even when they were playing in the school yard. David Lloyd George's uncle,

Richard Lloyd was deaf in one ear because he had been hit on the head by a teacher for speaking Welsh at school.

Throughout the 20th century, the number of Welsh speakers continued to decline. One of the reasons the flooding of Capel Celyn was so upsetting for the Welsh was that the village was a first language Welsh-speaking community.

The Welsh Language Society (*Cymdeithas Yr Iaith Cymraig*) was set up in 1962 to encourage more people to use the language. The fate of the Welsh language was always linked to the political wish for more independence from England.

In 1966, *Plaid Cymru*, the Welsh National Party, won their first seat in Westminster. The man who won it, Gwynfor Evans fought passionately for the Welsh language. In 1980, he said he would go on hunger strike if Margaret Thatcher's government did not set up a Welsh-speaking TV channel as they had promised. In 1982, S4C was set up and still transmits Welsh programmes, including news and even "soaps"[1] in Welsh.

The Welsh Language Act of 1993 gave Welsh the same importance as English in Wales. Since 1999, all children in Wales learn Welsh until the age of 16. About one fifth of all schools in Wales are so-called "Welsh-medium", meaning that subjects are taught in Welsh.

Welsh is still only spoken by around 20% of the population but the Welsh government has an ambitious goal: one million Welsh-speakers by 2050.

---

1. soap operas are TV dramas about everyday life.

VISIT WALES VII

CARDIFF

Cardiff is a relatively young capital city. It became Wales's capital in 1955. It is small but there are lots of things to do and visit here. Cardiff has the **Millenium Stadium** where international rugby and football matches are held.

You can visit **Cardiff Castle** with its Roman walls, a tower from the 11th century and the main castle building which was restored in the 19th century by the Marquis of Bute. Bute also restored the medieval castle in the north of the city, **Castell Coch** (Red Castle).

Cardiff is home to the **Museum of Wales** where you can learn about the history of Wales and visit the city's art collection.

From the city, you can take a boat trip down to **Cardiff Bay**. In the 19th century, coal was transported from Cardiff Bay all over the world. In 1999, a barrage was built which created a freshwater lake and the whole area was re-developed. It is now *the* place to go for a walk around the bay and then go for something to eat in one of the many restaurants.

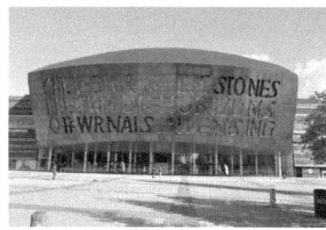

Cardiff Bay is also the home of the **Wales Millennium Centre**, an impressive theatre made of local slate and copper-coloured steel. The front of the theatre has two lines of a poem, one line in Welsh and the next in English:

Creu gwir fel gwydr o ffwrnais awen
(Creating truth, like glass, from the furnace of inspiration)
In these stones horizons sing

The **Welsh Parliament Building (Senedd Cymru)** is next door. It was opened on St David's Day 2006. The building is made of Welsh slate and oak and was built to be environmentally friendly and sustainable. Above the chamber where the representatives meet, there is a funnel. It lets light into the chamber and at the same time allows fresh air to be drawn in. The building is made of glass to let in as much natural light as possible and automatic windows open to control the temperature in the building. The glass also shows that the work of the parliament is transparent for the people. The building uses a biomass boiler for heat in the winter and rainwater is collected to flush the toilets and to maintain the building.[1]

Also in the Bay are the red-brick **Pierhead Building** which used to be the offices for the Bute Dock Company, the **Norwegian Church** where the writer Roald Dahl was christened and which is now an arts centre and **Techniquest**, the technology museum.

Senedd

---

1. You can take a virtual tour of the Senedd here
   https://senedd.wales/visit/things-to-do/virtual-tour/

WELSH LANGUAGE – BONUS

Take a look at the photo of the bottle bank on the last page. What do you notice?

The bottle bank is in Wales and there are three holes for different colour glass with the names in Welsh. You may guess that *clir* is clear or white glass and I can tell you that *gwyrdd* is green. But you may be surprised to see that the "Welsh" word for brown is ... *brown*!

There is an interesting reason for this. The names for colours always develop in the same way in every language. However, different languages are at different points in this development. For example, the languages in Papua New Guinea distinguish between light and dark but many of them have no other words for colours.

This is because black and white (or light and dark) always come first. The third colour to be named is always red. The fourth and fifth are either yellow or green, the sixth is blue and the seventh is brown. Modern Welsh only got as far as blue – it does not have a word for brown.

SOLUTIONS

On page 38, we looked at loanwords in Welsh. Did you guess what they were? Here are the solutions

- tacsi = taxi
  Welsh does not have a letter for "x" but "cs" sound like "x".

- ambwlans = ambulance

- car = car (obviously!)

- ffôn = phone
  Welsh does not have "ph" and uses "ff" instead. A single "f" is live "v" in English

- siop = shop
  In Welsh, "si" is pronounced like "sh" in English

- coffi = coffee
  An "i" at the end of a word is like the English "ee"

EXTRAS

Visit my blog to see colour photos of the pictures included in this book and information about the travel tips. You can also find some links to websites where you can hear people speaking Welsh.

https://sarahcurtiusbooks.wordpress.com/wales/

ABOUT THE AUTHOR

Sarah Curtius is an English teacher who lives near Hanover in Germany. She studied German and English in the UK and Germany and in 2019, she completed her MA in Applied Linguistics and TESOL (Teaching English to Speakers of Other Languages).

When she is not encouraging people to learn English, she loves to paint, sew and do any kind of handicraft. She is proud of her homeland of Wales which is the most beautiful place on earth!

ALSO BY SARAH CURTIUS

**WHO ARE YOU
CALLING OLD?**

SARAH CURTIUS

WHO ARE YOU CALLING OLD?

How old is 'old'? Do *you* feel old? What happens to us as we get older? Read about some inspiring people and find out about what happens in our brain as we age and why learning new skills is still possible. (CEFR Level B1)

ISBN: 978-3-7543-3070-8

SHAKESPEARE: STORIES FOR TODAY

In this book you will find stories based on Shakespeare's plays and his characters. Meet Bottom from "A Midsummer Night's Dream", the young lovers from "The Merchant of Venice", and the twins separated after a shipwreck from "Twelfth Night". (CEFR Level B1/B2)

ISBN: 978-3-756-832-552

Read a page of English every day in December! Learn about the history of Christmas, Christmas songs, British Christmas traditions, Christmas fairy tales, and do some puzzles.
(CEFR Level B1)

ISBN: 978-3-756-863-174

Order the books in your local bookshop or here
https://www.bod.de/buchshop/

COMING SOON

The History Series

Books about British history for English learners (CEFR B1).

As well as the lives of well-known personalities, find out what was happening in science and culture, what everyday life was like and read about a scandal or two.

The first book in the series will look at the times of the
Tudor Kings.

Who are the Tudors?
Who was the first woman to publish a book?
Who invented the first watch?

ACKNOWLEDGEMENTS

To my Welsh mam, Doreen and my honorary Welsh husband, Christoph – thank you for proofreading and for your tips.

PHOTO CREDITS